THE PRESENT ABANDONED

poems by

Harriet L. Shenkman

Finishing Line Press
Georgetown, Kentucky

THE PRESENT ABANDONED

for
Jerry, Ethan, Hartley and Jordana

Copyright © 2020 by Harriet L. Shenkman
ISBN 978-1-64662-182-8 First Edition
All rights reserved under International and Pan-American Copyright Conventions. No part of this book may be reproduced in any manner whatsoever without written permission from the publisher, except in the case of brief quotations embodied in critical articles and reviews.

ACKNOWLEDGMENTS

Grateful acknowledgement is made for poems published in slightly different versions and under different titles.

Women's National Book Association Annual Edition of National Contest Winners, 2013—"Reflection" appeared as "Mirror, Mirror."
Oyez Review, Roosevelt University, Winter 2017—"A Simple List" appeared as "Dementia."
Alexandria Quarterly, Fall, 2018, "Unfettered" appeared as "The Wrenching."
The Comstock Review, "Shells" accepted March, 2020

I am exceedingly appreciative of the help and influence of teachers, editors and readers: Jennifer Franklin, Laura Kasischke, Ellaraine Lockie, David Rigsbee, Diane Schenker and Tamra Carraher. I am also grateful to Kathline Carr for her art work.

I am eternally grateful to my family for accompanying me on a difficult journey.

Publisher: Leah Maines
Editor: Christen Kincaid
Cover Art: *Climbing the Fracture Zone,* Kathline Carr, www.kathlinecarr.com
Author Photo: Jordana Shenkman
Cover Design: Tamra Carraher

Printed in the USA on acid-free paper.
Order online: www.finishinglinepress.com
        also available on amazon.com

Author inquiries and mail orders:
Finishing Line Press
P. O. Box 1626
Georgetown, Kentucky 40324
U. S. A.

Table of Contents

I.

African Market 1

The Reckoning 2

Jazz Buff 3

Not Guilty 4

A Simple List 5

Happy Nail Salon 6

These Beauties 7

Morning 8

Two Artists 9

Our Rooms 10

The Ladies 11

Reflection 12

Shells 13

II.

Dementia Unit 17

The Present Abandoned 18

A Resort 19

Shooting Pool 20

Rummy 21

Egg Collage 22

The Other Woman 23

Unfettered 24

Madame Tussauds 25

Modigliani Exhibit 26

Venice 27

There is a crack in everything.
That's how the light gets in.

Leonard Cohen

I.

AFRICAN MARKET

In a Senegal market, vendors
stand on corners, cages crammed

with red-billed finches.
If someone buys a finch and lets it go,

people say it will fly away
with their pain. The price varies

with the gravity of the sorrow.
I'd give a fortune for a finch that soars

into the sky clutching my despair
when I see you raise your arm

to slap yourself as if a naughty child.

THE RECKONING

You shook hands with Yogi Berra at spring training, caught a paper bag with bread and butter thrown down five stories by your grandma, loved sausage biscuits and grits, received oral sex from a girl who peed in the sink, listened intently to Al Cohen and Zoot Sims on our first date, swung a shovel at me when reminded to finally rake our gravel driveway, explained the subtleties of *mens rea*, braved an ice storm to rescue our young daughter, negotiated by giving in, lost at the racetrack and won at Chinese checkers. Now, you gaze at your life stretched out like a hand before you in a blizzard.

JAZZ BUFF

John Coltrane   and Miles,
your favorites.

You tap out   syncopated beats
on tabletops and dashboards.

At 3 a.m. you scat   an Ella tune,
jolting me from sleep.

You click quarter notes   with your tongue,
beat in time to the hedge clippers

and hum to oil sputtering   in the frying pan,
flick the wine glass raised

to bless the fruit   of the vine.
Four four, four four, four four.

Dooo   AAAAH!   Dooo   AAAAH!

NOT GUILTY

Last night the cupcakes went missing,
four in a variety of flavors, chocolate,

French vanilla, key lime and red velvet.
As innocent as a newborn, you can't

remember getting up from bed,
stealing into the kitchen and pulling open

the refrigerator door despite a trail
of crumbs leading to your side of the bed.

You'll plead not guilty and I'll have to shake off
my anger to offer you a pardon

even if the turkey drumsticks disappear
and the frozen potpies are cracked open.

A SIMPLE LIST

I send you to CVS
for two rolls of toilet paper,
dandruff shampoo and a pint
of vanilla ice cream.

In the hair products aisle,
you stop a blonde
with a mess of curls,
ask for the best shampoo.

She smiles and points
to a shimmering tube,
invites you to admire her
silky hair in the shower.

At the dairy freezer,
nothing much happens,
the toilet paper aisle,
another matter.

You are deciding
between cushioned
and razor-thin when
a man with side locks

approaches you, eager
to wrap a leather strap
up your arm and place
a box on your forehead.

You both recite a prayer
and linking your arms,
dance past the antacids,
into the pain-relief aisle.

HAPPY NAIL SALON

Select a color, please.
Demure Vixen? Surrender at Sunset?
I see myself in black turtleneck, heading

to our first Greenwich Village date.

Nice day, no? The manicurist files expertly,
buffs each nail. Then she reaches
for my arm and the tube of cream,

the half-minute massage over too soon.

Cut cuticles? she asks. *No, push back.*
You tap on the storefront window
and I turn away,

not the partner I'd hoped to be.

The manicurist cradles each finger,
applies a clear liquid, shakes the tiny
bottle and brushes on the polish

in tender mini strokes.

Please sit, fifteen minutes to dry.
Next to the wall clock, a print
of Van Gogh's giant sunflowers.

How long before he went mad?

You tap at the window again.
I spring up and reach out, my nails
a mess of bumps and streaks now.

THESE BEAUTIES

We stroll through the local market.
I cradle a dozen roses in my arms,
deep coral petals nestling tender buds,

an unbearable sweetness in the air.

How nice, a passing neighbor remarks,
Is it your anniversary?

Turning to you, I say,
Thank you for these beauties,

though I buy them for myself.

MORNING

You hold a piece of buttered toast
and bite down carefully. *Don't you remember,*
you say, upper lip caked with crumbs,
you proposed to me.

TWO ARTISTS

You were the fine artist, making
tiny dabs of cream cheese with your knife,
a pointillist, covering every bit
of your bagel's surface, the interior circle
carefully sculpted.

I was the *schmearer*, flinging globs
of pinkish salmon spread, overlapping
a white whip laced with chives,
edges of the round canvas rough
and unmanicured.

OUR ROOMS

Near the front door, an inlaid copper *hamsa*, the hand
meant to keep misfortune at bay.

    And inside a polished walnut cabinet,

a jug thrown by a Carolina potter with arthritic thumbs.
Racks of record albums line the shelves, Miles abutting Mozart.

    Between two casement windows,

hangs a child's drawing of a three-legged camel
basking under clouds and a black sun.

    On the mantel in the dining room,

sits a Roman style wine goblet,
the one we leave for Elijah each year.

    And in the bedroom off a hallway,

La Sinagoga di Firenze enveloped in fog covers a wall
and from a dresser, three children smile in silver frames.

    A marbled kitchen countertop

holds our Mr. Coffee pot, the one that brews
medium roast the way we like it.

    And in a sunlit alcove behind the kitchen,

the Salvador Dali clock ticks, our lives
melting off the shelf like a slice of cheese.

THE LADIES

We wait, impatient for the van to arrive.

The ladies are after me, you say the mornings
you go off to daycare like a preschooler.

You're sure one of the ladies will invite you up to her
place for coffee or maybe something more.

As the white van approaches, you turn to me.
I always refuse. None of them compares to you.

REFLECTION

You search my face, admire
the curve of my cheek, my image

reflected in your gaze.
I am desperate to string a photo of me

to wear around your neck, soak
your shirt collar in *Rive Gauche*,

turn myself into a Warhol print, twelve
versions of me plastered

on your wall. I'll encourage
you to lick my fingertips, taste

my essence in a roux. I will recite
my name in rhyme, because

how will I know myself,
if you can't remember me?

SHELLS

You and I walk along the beach gathering
a handful of shells, bleached fossil-like remnants,

bone-dry and carved in petrified swirls, punctured
in patterns that would please Michelangelo.

They bring to mind shells cracked open, ushering
newborns into the light. And there's also the shell

of a rifle's bullet after the quick death of prey,
not the withering that befalls you now, a slow

leak of matter, your brain calcifying without mercy.
Miles of white sand, rimmed by sea and sky, stretch

before us. You turn your unshaded eyes toward me,
Where are we going? you ask.

I don't know, I say.

II.

II

DEMENTIA UNIT

You and the rumpled lady sit at the table
      and scream at each other.

Stop drumming on the table, she yells.
      I am not, you dog.
You're a dirt bag, she mutters.
      No, I'm not, you whore.

And when it grows dark, you bang on all
      the doors, seeking a way out.

It's the music in you, I know. You are a jazz
      drummer in your soul.

Your unscreened self has taken over, a person
      I hardly recognize.

THE PRESENT ABANDONED

Minutes ago are abandoned while
        you dangle in the morning air,
grasping for an elusive context.

You invite me to ramble in your distant past,
        an unwilling voyeur. You are gambling
at the racetrack with uncle Jack, peeing

in Roanne's sink late at night,
        slipping a bill into the fringed boot of
the Go-Go girl dancing on the tabletop.

You are now listening to the Russian chatter
        at the Indonesian Embassy as a mist
rises to engulf the domed Capitol.

A RESORT

There are fake plants and a carpet of aqua and white flowers.

> Even a bistro with a poker table and a pool table
> with cue sticks on the second floor.

When you see me, you slide into our former life,

> glad we're vacationing at a resort, but will soon
> pack our bags, get in the car and go home.

We eat sugar-free cookies, drink apple juice

> through straws. We take out *New York Monopoly*,
> a game we used to play with our children.

You roll the dice and I move the tokens around

> the board. You buy Central Park,
> Belmont Racetrack and decline Park Avenue.

I dole out the pastel money as you pass Go,

> but the worst is when it's time for me to leave,
> me slipping away without you knowing.

SHOOTING POOL

You chalk up the tip of the cue stick,
    arrange the solid-color and striped balls in a triangle.
    The white ball waits impatiently.

    Break!

Though I never saw you play in our years together,
    you know the positioning of fingers,
    which pocket to aim toward.

    Scratch!

You stage the white ball,
    move the striped ball blocking your aim, grip
    the cue stick, bend over the table and shoot.

    Point!

You look around the parlor.
    This pool hall is nice,
    less seedy than others I've been to.

    Eight ball!

RUMMY

The king of spades attacks with two swords
and the queen of hearts offers her sprig of flowers.

Trouble and love, a heady mix.

Deal. Seven, not eight, cards.
You spread the cards in your hand.

I throw out a two-of-clubs.

Rummy you declare, though you're missing
a queen-of-diamonds. I used to play with my dad,

admire the four queens with their dour faces.

Whichever way they turned, they remained the same.
My dad let me win most games, both of us delighted

as the pennies piled high to the rim of my jar.

Now, when you fan out your cards on the table,
I shout in a cheery voice, *You win,*

and toss a few pennies onto your pile.

EGG COLLAGE

Arts and crafts were not your strong suit.
In biology class, you wrote the reports

and your friend Howie drew the diagrams.

Today, you are offered scraps of pastel-colored paper
for pasting Easter eggs in a cut-out yellow basket.

You never once celebrated the rebirth of Jesus

or excelled at kindergarten tasks, though you could
recite due process laws and name the far-flung capitols

of Africa. Now, you pick up a pink oval shape and slant

it over the yellow basket. As if you just walked on water,
you point proudly to the collage before you

and I try hard to glue a pastel smile on my lips.

THE OTHER WOMAN

You twirl around with Gloria,
waltzing to a rumba beat.

Because you were only a so-so dancer,
I always felt the need to lead.

You would listen intently to the beat,
but your torso never followed.

Now you dance around the room in a happy fog,
and pausing for an instant, you turn to me.

I won't do it again, you say,
and I dismiss your confession with a wave.

UNFETTERED

We may have to go down
our separate paths and not be terrified.

Content in the moment, you hold hands with a petite
woman whose hair was once as brown as mine.

Go there, come here, Gloria, and she follows easily,
unlike me, who used to practice resistance.

You are unfettered and in command, and I am the matador,
 slipping aside gracefully as you glide into the dust.

MADAME TUSSAUDS

The wax figures of Angelina and Brad were split apart
at Madame Tussauds following the recent announcement
of their divorce. They were positioned at a respectful distance.

What will mark our severing?

I doubt darkness will descend for a day and a night
or the sea will part as it did for the ancient Israelites.
Most likely, there will be the swish of a tea bag in hot water.

MODIGLIANI EXHIBIT

I always admired Amedeo's elongated necks,
unseeing eyes and reclining nudes.

    Lola, Adrienne and Jeanne gaze back at me,
woman to woman,

    and you are the ghost hovering.

Music was your love, not paintings, yet
you tagged along when I toured the galleries.

    Now, I linger at a portrait of Anna Akhmatova
and stop before the Greek caryatids,

    sensing you meandering through the rooms.

We were a couple once, part of the admiring crowd.
I was not the solitary stranger

    envious of the pair beside me, his hand
reaching up to touch the nape of her neck,

    unaware they are the exhibit.

VENICE

I stand on the Bridge of Sighs,
and grieve, not for a last glimpse
of the city as prisoners did, but

for the sight of you as you once were,

clear-eyed, two years over twenty,
dense presidential hair,
a white rose bud in your lapel, eager

to break the glass beneath your foot.

Harriet L. Shenkman was born in Brooklyn and earned a Ph.D. from Fordham University and an M.Ed. from Duke University. She is a Professor Emerita at City University of New York and serves on the Advisory Board of the Women's National Book Association, NYC. Her poetry awards include the Women's National Book Association 2013 Annual Writing Contest in Poetry, The Women Who Write 2013 International Poetry and Short Prose Contest and The Raynes Poetry Competition, 2014 finalist. Her poetry appeared in *Union, Evening Street Review, Third Wednesday, Jewish Currents, Jewish Magazine, Jewish Quarterly, VerseWrights.com., When Women Awaken, The Westchester Review. Oyez Review, The Pink Panther Magazine, The Calliope Anthology and The Alexandria Quarterly*. A Poet-in-Residence at The Transition Network, she studied with poets Jennifer Franklin, Ellen Bass and Laura Kasischke. She read her poetry at the Hudson Valley Poetry Center, KGB Bar, Cornelia Street Café, The Arc Poetry and Art Festival, The JCC of Mid Westchester, The Watercooler Hub in Tarrytown, The Scarsdale Library and The Westchester Review at Barnes and Noble. Her first chapbook *Teetering* was published by Finishing Line Press in 2014.

www.ingramcontent.com/pod-product-compliance
Lightning Source LLC
LaVergne TN
LVHW041509070426
835507LV00012B/1438